Food
APPLES

Louise Spilsbury

Heinemann Library
Chicago, Illinois

Designed by Celia Floyd
Illustrated by Tokay Interactive
Originated by Ambassador Litho
Printed by South China Printing Co. in Hong Kong

05 04 03 02 01
10 9 8 7 6 5 4 3 2 1

Library of Congress Cataloging-in-Publication Data
Spilsbury, Louise.
   Apples / Louise Spilsbury.
      p. cm. -- (Food)
Includes bibliographical references and index.
   ISBN 1-58810-142-8 (library binding)
   1. Apples--Juvenile literature. 2. Cookery (Apples)--Juvenile
literature. [1. Apples.] I. Title. II. Series.
   TX558.A6 S65 2001
   641.3'411--dc21
                            00-012517

Acknowledgments
The Publishers would like to thank the following for permission to reproduce photographs:
Amazone, p. 16; Corbis, pp. 8, 12, Paul Seheult/Corbis, p. 21, Michael S. Yamashita/Corbis, pp. 18, 19, Ed Young/Corbis, p. 20; Gareth Boden, pp. 6, 7, 22, 23, 25, 28, 29; Image Bank, p. 24; Mike Slater/Oxford Scientific Films, p. 17; Peter Newark's American Pictures, p. 9; J. Luke/PhotoDisc, p. 14; Roger Scruton, p. 15, Roger Scruton/Photoshop, p. 13; James Darell/Tony Stone, p. 4, Jake Rais/Tony Stone, p. 5, Andy Sacks/Tony Stone, p. 11.

Our thanks to the American Farm Bureau Federation for their comments in the preparation of this book.

Cover photograph reproduced with permission of Gareth Boden.

Every effort has been made to contact copyright holders of any material reproduced in this book. Any omissions will be rectified in subsequent printings if notice is given to the publisher.

Some words are shown in bold, **like this.** You can find out what they mean by looking in the glossary.

Contents

What Are Apples?

Apples are a kind of **fruit** that we can eat. People eat more apples than any other fruit in the world.

Apples grow on trees. Most of the apples we eat are grown in orchards. Orchards are pieces of land where many fruit trees grow.

Kinds of Apples

There are thousands of different kinds of apples. You can divide them into two main kinds—dessert and cooking apples. Dessert apples taste sweet. You can eat them **raw.**

Cooking apples are hard. They taste **sour** if you eat them raw. You need to cook them before you can eat them.

In the Past

The **Romans** grew apple trees so they could eat the **fruit.** They planted orchards in Europe. This Roman **mosaic** shows a bird on an apple.

English people took apple **seeds** to America 300 years ago. Later, a famous man known as "Johnny Appleseed" traveled all over the country. He gave away and planted apple seeds.

Around the World

This map shows some of the countries that grow the most apples. Apples grow best in countries that have warm summers and chilly winters.

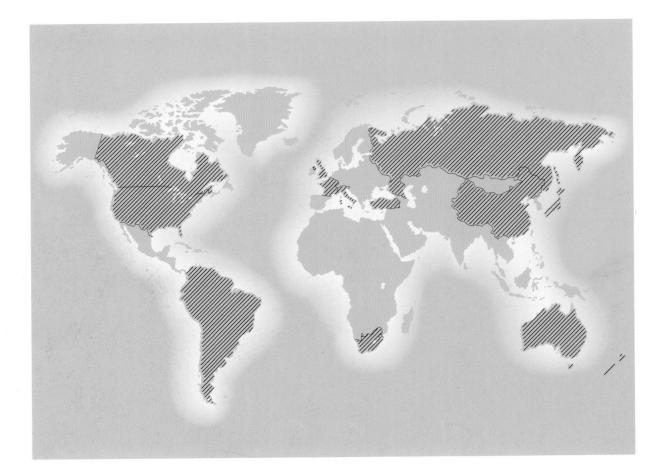

China grows more apples than any other country. The United States grows many apples, too.

Looking at Apples

Like all plants, apple trees need water, **nutrients,** and sunlight to grow. Roots take in water and nutrients from the soil. The branches hold up the leaves to reach light.

leaves

branch

trunk

roots
(these are
mostly
underground)

12

Inside an apple, the **core** holds the **seeds.** The stalk is the part that attaches the apple to the tree. We can eat the flesh and the **peel.**

stalk   peel   flesh   seeds

core

Apple Trees

In spring, apple trees grow flowers. Bees fly to the flowers. When the bees drink **nectar** from the flowers, yellow **pollen** clings to their bodies.

The bees land on different trees. The pollen rubs off onto their flowers. The pollen makes new **seeds** grow in these flowers. The apple **fruit** begins to grow around these seeds.

Growing Apples

Apples grow in summer. Some farmers feed the trees with **fertilizers.** Fertilizers help the trees grow big, juicy apples.

Many farmers also spray the trees with **pesticides.** These sprays stop insects from eating and spoiling the apples.

Picking Apples

In autumn, the apples are ready to eat. Most apples are picked by hand because they **bruise** easily. Farmers keep apple trees short so the apples are easy to reach.

The apples are washed in big machines. Then, farmers store the apples in very cold rooms. This keeps them fresh until the farmers sell them.

Apples to Buy

Before going to **consumers,** apples are sorted by hand. Damaged ones are thrown away. Then the good apples are sorted into different sizes by a machine.

The apples are packed into smaller boxes. In between the layers is soft paper. This keeps the apples from knocking against each other.

Eating Apples

Raw apples can be eaten by themselves or put in **fruit** salads. Cooked apples can be used as a **side dish.**

Apples are also **processed** in different ways. They may be used in jam with other fruits, as fruit pie fillings, or in jellies. Apples are also used to make fruit juices.

Good for You

Apples contain **nutrients** that give you energy and keep you healthy. They also contain **vitamins** that help your body grow and **protect** you from illness.

Apple **peel** is good for you. Apple peel contains **fiber.** As fiber passes through your body, it keeps your **digestive system** clean and healthy.

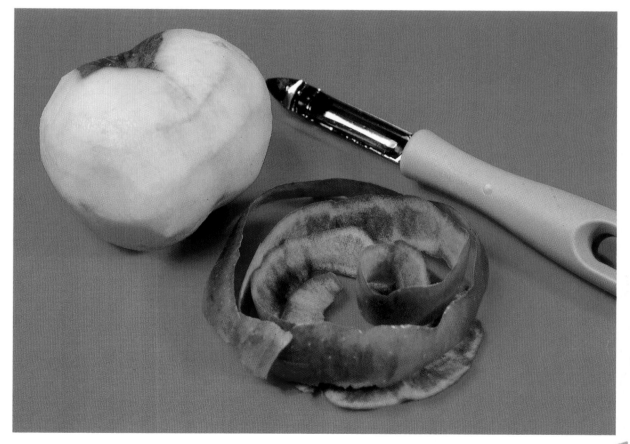

Healthy Eating

The food guide **pyramid** shows how much of each different kind of food you should eat every day.

All of the food groups are important, but your body needs more of some foods than others.

You should eat more of the foods at the bottom and the middle of the pyramid. You should eat less of the foods at the top.

Apples are in the **fruit** group. Your body needs two servings of fruit each day.

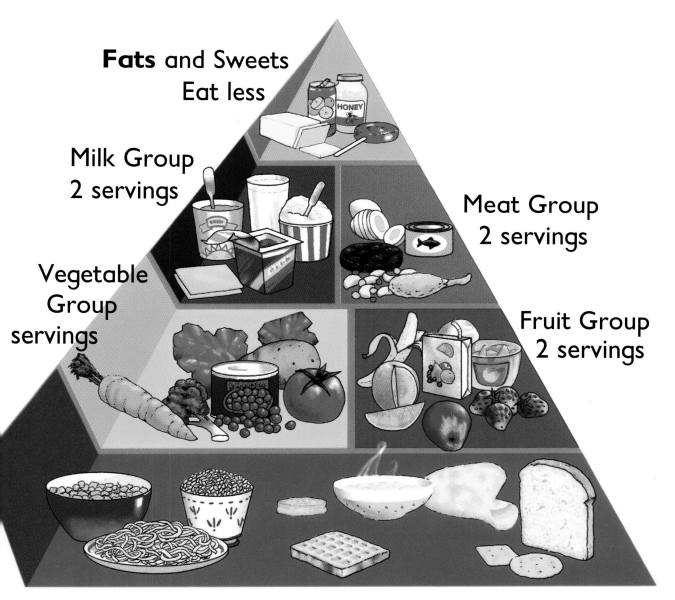

Fats and Sweets
Eat less

Milk Group
2 servings

Meat Group
2 servings

Vegetable
Group
servings

Fruit Group
2 servings

Grain Group   6 servings

Based on the Food Guide Pyramid for Young Children, U.S. Department of
Agriculture, Center for Nutrition Policy and Promotions, March 1999.

27

Applesauce Recipe

1. Cut the **peel** off the apples and chop them into pieces.

2. Put the pieces into a pan and cover with water.

3. Cook gently until the apple is soft.

You will need:
- 2 large apples
- water
- spoonful of honey
- pinch of cinnamon

Ask an adult to help you!

4. Pour the cooked apple into a blender.

5. Blend until you have made a smooth sauce. Add the honey and a little cinnamon.

6. Serve the sauce warm or cold.

Glossary

bruise mark caused when fruit is handled roughly

consumer person who buys things he or she needs or wants, like food

core hard, center part of a fruit that holds the seeds

digestive system part of your body that breaks down food into tiny bits

fat part of some foods that the body uses to get energy and to keep warm

fertilizer spray or powder that helps plants grow bigger and produce more fruit

fiber rough part of a plant that passes through our bodies when we eat it

fruit part of a plant that grows around the seeds

grain seed of a cereal plant

mosaic small pieces of stone or pottery put together to make a picture

nectar sweet juice in the center of a flower

nutrient food that plants or people need to grow and be healthy

peel thin outside of a fruit

pesticide spray farmers use to kill insects and other creatures that damage crops

pollen tiny yellow specks on a flower that help make seeds

processed food that is cooked or treated in a certain way to make a new kind of food or drink

protect to keep safe

pyramid shape with a flat bottom and three sides with edges that come to a point

raw not cooked

Roman person from Rome, Italy. Long ago, Romans ruled over many lands, including much of Europe.

seed the part of a plant that can grow into a new plant

side dish food served to go along with the main part of a meal

sour not sweet

vitamin something that the body needs to grow and stay healthy

More Books to Read

Royston, Angela. *Flowers, Fruits, and Seeds*. Chicago: Heinemann Library, 1999.

Royston, Angela. *Life Cycle of an Apple*. Chicago: Heinemann Library, 1998.

Saunders-Smith, Gail. *Apples*. Danbury, Conn.: Children's Press, 1998.

Ward, Kristin. *Apples*. New York: Rosen Publishing Group, 2000.

Index